Illustrator:
Phil Hopkins

Editor:
Evan D. Forbes, M.S. Ed.

Editor in Chief:
Sharon Coan, M.S. Ed.

Art Director:
Elayne Roberts

Associate Designer:
Denise Bauer

Cover Artist:
Marc Kazlauskas

Product Manager:
Phil Garcia

Imaging:
Ralph Olmedo, Jr.

Acknowledgements:
ClarisWorks is a registered trademark of Apple Computer, Inc.

Screen shot(s) and other images reprinted with permission from Microsoft Corporation.

HyperStudio® is a registered trademark of Roger Wagner Publishing.

Publishers:
Rachelle Cracchiolo, M.S. Ed.
Mary Dupuy Smith, M.S. Ed.

TECHNOLOGY CONNECTIONS

FOR

Westward Movement

INTERMEDIATE

Author:

Kathleen N. Kopp, M.S. Ed.

Teacher Created Materials, Inc.
6421 Industry Way
Westminster, CA 92683
www.teachercreated.com

©1997 Teacher Created Materials, Inc.
Reprinted, 1999
Made in U.S.A.

ISBN-1-57690-206-4

Table of Contents

Computer Integration: An Introduction

Using This Book

Technology Connections for Westward Movement was created with you in mind. Perhaps you are an avid user of computer programs and related technology. Possibly you are somewhat proficient in the ways of technology and wish to get to know how to use a computer more effectively, but you lack the time or know-how to even get started. Or maybe you are one of many in this technologically advanced society who still shies away from computers altogether; you have no knowledge of computers, and the idea of using computers with your students scares you half out of your wits! Whoever you are, this book is for you. From the most proficient to the least knowledgeable, you can now integrate the use of computers and related technology with your students into your everyday curriculum.

Most of us are probably somewhere in the middle as far as computer literacy is concerned. We may type here and there at home or at school. We may use computers with our students in the most popular way, playing games. We want to teach our students the myriad of purposeful applications computers have to offer, but this takes time (which we all know teachers have little enough of already), and we may lack the most rudimentary knowledge: where to begin. In addition, teaching computer literacy in itself without purpose or long-range objectives seems a waste of time. What we need is the ideal situation—ideas to teach computer skills by integrating meaningful computer activities into our existing curriculum. This book will do that for us.

This book offers integrated computer projects your students can complete. They are meant to complement topics about the Westward Movement that you may already teach your students; they are not units in and of themselves. **The activities are designed to be used with various word processing, desktop publishing, and multimedia computer programs you may use in your school, specifically** *ClarisWorks* **(word processing),** *Creative Writer* **(desktop publishing), and** *HyperStudio* **(multimedia). Many software companies are now publishing numerous comparable programs which may act as substitutes for the former. If your school doesn't have** *Creative Writer*, **for example, you can still implement the activities with an alternative creative writing or desktop publishing program such as** *Print Shop* **or** *SuperPrint*.

All you need to know to help your students successfully complete the computer projects described in this book is how to access a program, open files saved to disk, and click and drag the mouse. Refer to the program basics sections to familiarize yourself with the programs you may not feel comfortable using. When you see words that are **bolded**, that means to click on those directional cues. Some directions have two **bold...words** connected by three dots. You should click on the first direction, drag down, and release the mouse on the second. So the direction **File...Save** means to click on "File," drag down to "Save," and then release.

The time necessary to complete these projects adjusts to your schedule. Your students may complete them in one hour or one week, depending on the availability of computer usage, your students' knowledge of the programs you use, and the length of the project.

Read through the activities to decide which ones are right for you. Then hop on that computer and type away.

Technology All Around Us

Computers and computer-related technology have steadfastly become an integral part of our everyday lives. As consumers, a great portion of our purchases is made using technology.

We find it at the grocery store, the gas station, restaurants, etc. It's in hotels, laundromats, and car washes. Challenge yourself to live one day—or even half a day—without the use of advanced technology. You may think you can hide out at the beach and let one day in the age of technology pass you by. But consider your means of travel to and from the beach. Most of today's cars have computer chips monitoring their internal systems. If you consider riding your bike, think of the manner in which it was designed and marketed prior to its purchase. Walking? Civil engineers may have had a technological hand in designing the roads, sidewalks, or sewer systems upon which you tread. And what of the beach itself? Scientists are continually monitoring wave motions, tidal patterns, beach erosion, current weather trends, and sea life—all with the use of advanced technology.

Technology has also infiltrated our school systems. Payroll, food services, budget and finance, as well as other areas within a school or district, have begun to depend on computers to perform tasks and manage large amounts of information. Student records no longer take weeks to process. If a teacher feels specific information about a child is required immediately, he or she can simply request a fax of the necessary documents.

And what of the classroom itself? Computer and technology usage may vary from school to school, but chances are they all use some technological applications in some form or other. Your school may be one to use video technology to broadcast a live (or taped) morning show throughout the school. You may take advantage of multimedia programs such as *Oregon Trail* or *Point of View 2.0: An Overview of American History* to supplement your already outstanding curriculum on Westward Movement.

Yes, computers and computer-related technology are all around us. It is here now while our students are fairly young. It will be here when our students graduate and become productive members of society. And it will be here when our students' grandchildren are faced with their own set of technological advances. Things are moving so fast now, we can hardly keep up with the changes ourselves. A computer bought today may be archaic within the year. Regardless of the changes taking place now, we must still take the time to prepare our students for the world of technology they will encounter in their futures. The following pages and subsequent activities will answer the question of what we can do today to help our students learn for tomorrow.

Looking Ahead

Our jobs as educators have evolved to encompass a great quantity of subject matter. We are still required to teach the basics of yesterday yet are expected to also provide our students with the training and skills they will need to carry them through tomorrow's technological advancements. Computers are the tools to pave the way for our students' futures. With the use of computers, we can teach the skills students need to learn, model the role of technology in our society, and provide experiences necessary for their successes in life.

Few people would disagree that computer experiences are necessary in our schools so that our future leaders will be prepared to realize their dreams, regardless of the career choices they may decide upon for themselves. But more important than general computer knowledge is working computer knowledge. We, as educators, should be providing real-life experiences with today's advanced technology. But, more importantly, we should not lose sight of the ultimate goal: communication. Through the use of computers, we can open up a whole new world of communication for our students, provided that we supply the tools and skills necessary for its implementation.

Many of us realize the important role computers and computer-related technology will play in our students' futures. We also realize that we have a responsibility to our students to prepare them to utilize computers as learning tools and as an effective way of communicating with others. Nearly every school across the country undoubtedly uses computers in some manner or other to help teach students basic learning skills, as well as word processing skills. The beauty of today's technology is that we can now integrate skills learning with technology-related assignments and activities.

Today's computer programs can motivate students to greater achievements. Together, you and your students will use the power of computers to create astounding projects. Have fun!

Welcome to the Age of Technology!

With the use of computers, educators can . . .

- ◆ teach both academic and computer literacy skills
- ◆ model the role of technology
- ◆ provide real-life learning experiences
- ◆ teach students to communicate effectively

Integrated Applications Software: An Introduction

Most computer users are familiar with basic word processing applications. Word processing allows the typist much more freedom when creating a document. It used to be that when mistakes were made on a typewriter, the typist needed to start over. Not so with the help of today's technology. Word processing allows the writers to delete, add, change, style, and format their work, all with the touch of a few keys.

And if typing were not enough, many programs such as *ClarisWorks*, *Microsoft Works*, *WordPerfect*, etc., also include drawing, painting, database, and spreadsheet applications. This allows the user a variety of opportunities to enhance what was once just a typewritten piece of paper. For example, in the activity "Digging for Gold" you will be creating a treasure map using the word processing and paint application of your integrated application software.

ClarisWorks is a common integrated software program that utilizes word processing, drawing, painting, spreadsheet, database, and communications applications. This seemingly simple program can accomplish quite complicated word processing tasks if you know how to use the applications. Refer to "*ClarisWorks* Basics" to learn how to effectively use the basic applications *ClarisWorks* has to offer. Additional applications are described in the activities when they are called for. If you are generally familiar with this program or are using an alternative word processing program, take a look at the activities that accompany *Technology Connections for Westward Movement* in "Integrated Applications Software Activities."

ClarisWorks Basics

This is a brief guide through the word processing application of *ClarisWorks*. Refer to this section if you need assistance when implementing any of the *ClarisWorks* activities.

Word Processing

Upon opening the *ClarisWorks* folder, choose **Word Processing** and click **OK**. You will begin working on a new document. Type as you would on a typewriter. When you come to the end of a line, the computer will automatically return to the next line. Only use the return (enter) key on the keyboard when you want to start a new paragraph.

Task Bar Basics

You can select the line spacing, document layout, and alignment from the task bar that is displayed below the ruler. Clicking the **Body** box to the far right will allow you to choose other word processing options such as bullets, checklists, etc.

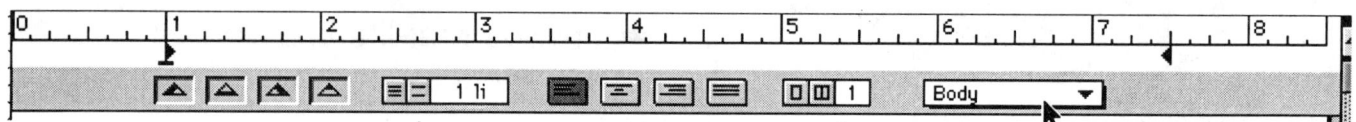

Increase or decrease line spacing

Alignment tools

Column guides

Integrated Applications Software: An Introduction *(cont.)*

ClarisWorks **Basics** *(cont.)*

Text Options

- You can change the type of letters you wish to use before you begin typing by clicking on **Font** and dragging to the type of letters you like.

- Clicking and dragging on **Size** will adjust the size of letters in your document.

- One final text option to consider is the style of letters (italics, bold, etc.). Click and drag **Style** to view the options available.

Spell Checker

If you wish to check your document spelling, click **Edit** and drag down to **Writing Tools...Check Document Spelling**. If the computer does not recognize a word in your document, it will offer alternatives. You can select one of the alternatives listed and click **Replace**. Or you can type the word you need in the box marked "Word:." If the word is correct but not in the computer database, choose **Skip** to tell the computer to overlook this word.

Editing

Chances are that once you have finished typing, you will wish to make some changes. The cursor is your way of communicating with the computer. You can move the cursor using the arrow keys to the text area you wish to change, or you can use the mouse to move the cursor to the appropriate place on the page and then click.

To edit text, move the cursor in front of the text you wish to edit. Clicking and dragging the text you wish to change will highlight it. Any changes you make will only be applied to this part of the text. This is useful if you wish to make headlines in a larger print or a different font and/or style.

To remove text, you can highlight it by clicking and dragging over it and then pressing the delete key. Or you can click the cursor in front of the text you wish to remove and press the delete key to erase the text one character at a time.

Quitting

Be sure to save your document before you quit. Go to **File...Save**. Choose the appropriate file in which you wish to place your document (either on the hard drive or on a disk). Then type in a name for this particular item. Click **Save**. The computer will save your document for you. Then you can **Quit** the program. When you wish to work on your document again, go to **File...Open**. Choose the file and click **Open** once again.

Activity 1: The Great Debate

Teacher Note: This project has been done using *ClarisWorks*. Any word processing program can be used, if properly modified.

Students apply critical thinking skills and practice word processing as they prepare arguments Monroe and Livingston may have presented to persuade France to sell New Orleans.

Background Knowledge: history of the Louisiana Purchase

Step 1: Setting the Stage

Display a map featuring the territorial growth of the United States. (See page 9.) Discuss the significance of the port of New Orleans. (*Settlers in the Ohio Valley shipped goods to prominent markets via the Ohio River to the Mississippi River; in an agreement with Spain, the United States was allowed to transfer goods without a fee from riverboats to ships at New Orleans for transport to Atlantic ports.*) Explain how France took control of the Louisiana Territory from Spain, it prohibited U.S. merchants from using the port of New Orleans. This led to an economic panic. Farmers were ready to take matters into their own hands by fighting the French for control of this city. Thomas Jefferson, then president, sent James Monroe to France to aid Robert R. Livingston in an attempt to peacefully buy the port from Napoleon. Fortunately, Napoleon faced political conflicts closer to home and agreed to sell the entire territory, including New Orleans. Jefferson acquired about eight thousand square miles for the United States for fifteen million dollars-—about three cents an acre.

Step 2: Persuading Napoleon

After a discussion of the Louisiana Purchase, have your students pretend to be either Monroe as he prepares to embark for France or Livingston. Students brainstorm at least five arguments they might use to persuade Napoleon to sell New Orleans to the United States. Then they use their brainstorming list to type a written proposal in *ClarisWorks*. Have your students practice using bullets to list their arguments (**Body...Bullets**). At the same time, assign two or three of your best debaters to play Napoleon. They brainstorm reasons why he should refuse the delegates' request and type a rejection letter in *ClarisWorks,* also using bullets to accentuate their points. Print the resulting proposals.

Step 3: Have a Debate

After all your students have their proposals ready, ask for volunteers to present their cases to one of the Napoleons. As the delegates confront Napoleon, the remainder of the class members check off the arguments already mentioned. Napoleon's job is to use his list to counter the points made by Monroe or Livingston. Trade delegates with other class members so that all students who wish to take part in the debate get a turn. At the end of the debate, have your class decide whose arguments were more compelling and who they would have sided with in 1803.

Activity 1: The Great Debate (cont.)

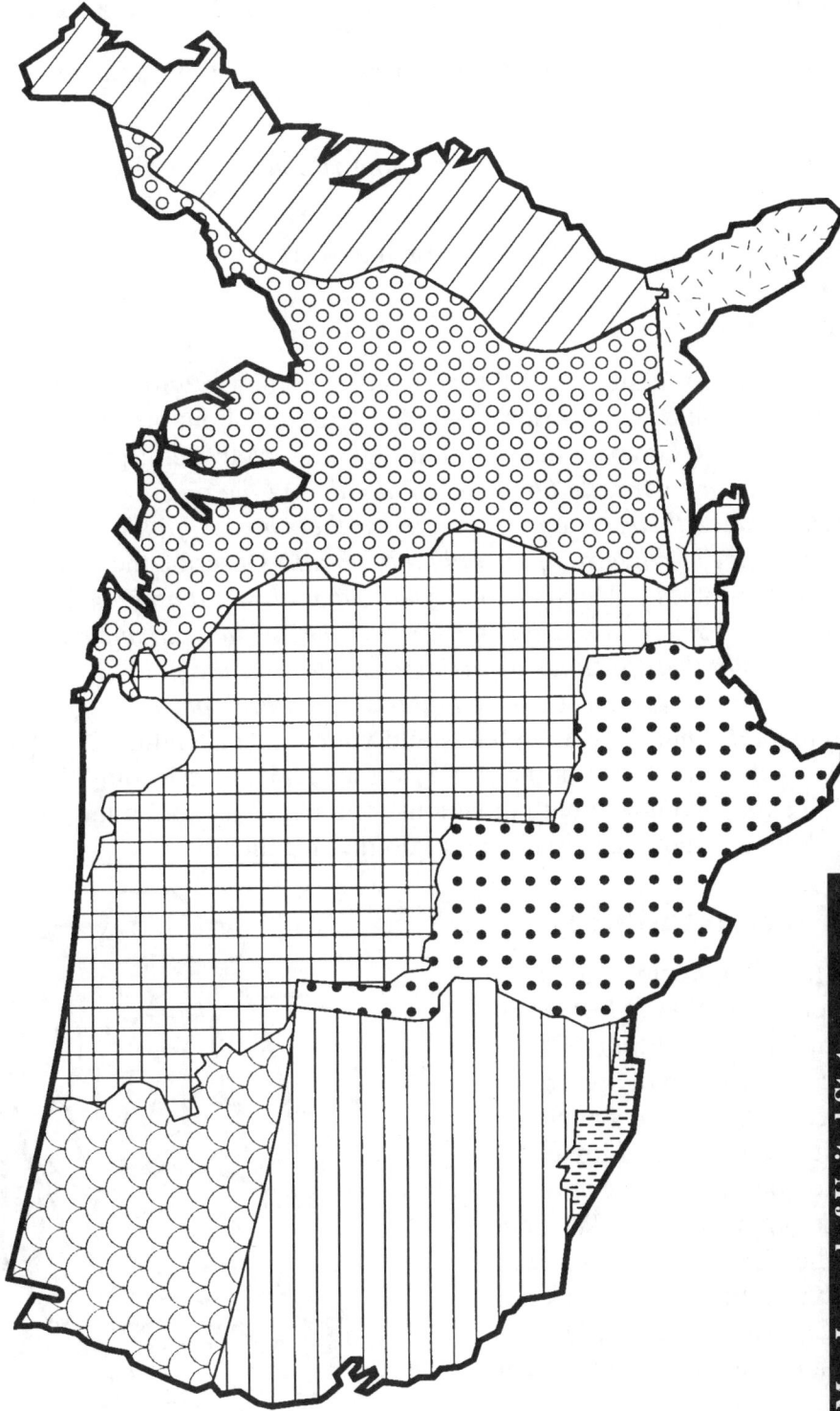

Map Legend of United States		
/	as of 1776	●	as of 1845
○	as of 1783		as of 1846
▢	as of 1803		as of 1848
	as of 1818		as of 1853
	as of 1819		

Activity 2: Digging for Gold

Teacher Note: This project has been done using *ClarisWorks*. Any paint, draw, and graphics program can be used, if properly modified.

Students apply their mapping skills by using the painting application of *ClarisWorks* to create a realistic map of a gold mine.

Background Knowledge: history of the Gold Rush, mapping skills

Step 1: Catch the Fever

If possible, dress as a miner may have dressed in the mid 1800s, complete with pan and pick. Ask your students if they ever wish they would strike it rich. Lead a discussion about how the students would go about finding a profitable mine and compare their present-day plans to those of gold seekers of 1849. (*Word of an abundance of gold mines traveled by word of mouth and the media. The stories were usually grossly exaggerated. Nevertheless, people abandoned their homes, families, and businesses and headed west to seek fortunes they had heard others only talk about.*) Describe the conditions gold seekers tolerated to find their fortunes. (*Mining camps were often crowded and unsanitary. Miners lived in tents, hastily constructed shacks, or in the open, sometimes without so much as a blanket for protection. Entrepreneurs sought their fortunes by taking advantage of the gold seekers. They sold their goods or services at exorbitant prices. Cramped quarters and high prices aside, gold diggers also fended off diseases, wild animals, and thieves.*) What would your students endure at a chance to strike it rich? Would they be more willing to "ride out the storm" if they had a map leading them to gold? Have your students sketch a map, complete with directions, of a fictitious gold mine. They should refrain from actually marking the spot—a classmate will do that for them.

Step 2: Create a Map in Painting

Have your students use their plan to create a map in the painting application of *ClarisWorks*. Instead of selecting Word Processing, select **Painting**. Click **OK**. To the far left of the page you will see the painting tools. Use these to create basic symbols. For more detailed graphics, select **File...Library**. Choose a topic suitable to your needs. View the picture you want by clicking on its name. When you find a picture you like, click **Use**. The graphic will appear on your field with marching ants. Click and drag the graphic where you want it. Close the library by clicking the open square in the upper-left corner of the dialog box.

Activity 2: Digging for Gold *(cont.)*

Working in Painting:

Shapes   Select the line, rectangle, rounded-corner rectangle, oval, or half circle to create these and similar shapes. The sideways square will make hexagons for you. Click and drag in the field to set the shape.

Odd shapes   Select the straight-sided polygon or curved-edge polygon to make odd shapes. Begin by clicking in the field. Move the mouse and click again to create a line. Each time you click, the mouse will stop drawing that line but continue to draw where you move the mouse. To stop drawing with this tool altogether, double-click.

Curved lines   Select the S-shaped tool to draw freehand curved lines. You must click and drag the mouse to create with this tool.

Colors   You can change the color, thickness, and pattern of the shapes' lines by selecting from the boxes under the pen at the bottom of the painting tools.

Painting   Select the paintbrush, pencil, or spray can to paint. Choose from a wide assortment of colors and patterns in the boxes below the paint can at the bottom of the painting tools. Choose the paint can from the toolbox to fill in any closed areas with a different color.

Typing   Select the large capital "A" to type in your document. You will first need to create a text field in which to type. Click and drag the mouse with the typing cursor to create a light-gray text area. When you let go of the mouse, you will see a blinking cursor in the text field. Select the font and size you wish to use before typing.

Editing   This application is not quite as user-friendly as the drawing application in that you cannot select items you wish to move or change with the select tool (or arrow). To edit a shape or text field, you must first select it. Choose the dotted box or the lasso. Click and drag a field around the item you wish to edit. Be careful that you only select the portion of your drawing you wish to edit. Any stray lines you may inadvertently select will be included in your edits. Notice the marching ants which appear around the object. Now the computer will allow you to make the changes you wish to make.

Click and drag items to move them to different locations on the map. Resize by selecting **Transform...Resize**. Delete objects by depressing the delete key.

You can also erase items by selecting the eraser. Selecting the magic wand and clicking on an object will select all adjacent items in an identical color.

Oops! Didn't want to do that? Immediately go to **Edit...Undo**. The computer will undo your last edit.

Activity 2: Digging for Gold *(cont.)*

Editing Tip: Draw the figures and text away from where you are working to make the editing process easier. Select the items to place them in the correct spots by lassoing them and then clicking and dragging them where they belong.

Painting Tools:

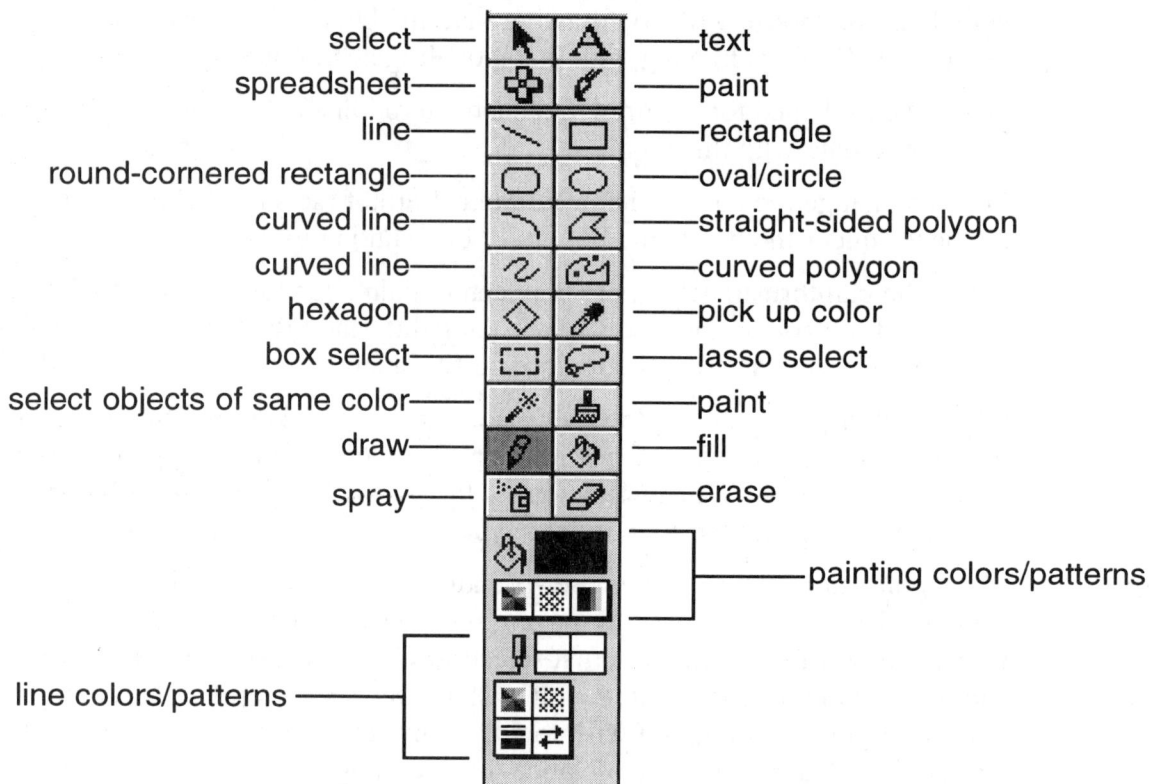

select	text
spreadsheet	paint
line	rectangle
round-cornered rectangle	oval/circle
curved line	straight-sided polygon
curved line	curved polygon
hexagon	pick up color
box select	lasso select
select objects of same color	paint
draw	fill
spray	erase

painting colors/patterns

line colors/patterns

Step 3: Print and Trade

Print your students' maps on parchment paper, if possible. Have each student trade maps with a classmate. The person reading the directions should draw a dotted line to mark the trail and place an X on the spot where he/she thinks the gold can be found. Have your students verify their marks with the mapmaker. Post your students' maps on a bulletin board entitled "Thar's Gold in Them Thar Hills!"

Activity 2: Digging for Gold *(cont.)*

Rielly's Gold Mine

Directions:

1. Start at Lado's Woods.
2. Go west through the mountains.
3. Head south to the shack.
4. Follow the river to Big Rock.
5. Ride north to Star Lake.
6. Dig on the east side of the lake.
7. Put an X to mark the spot.

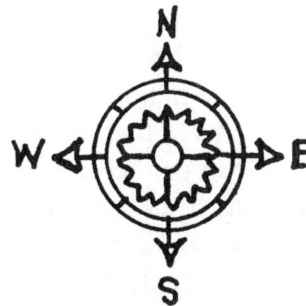

M A P	mountains	rock	lake
K E Y	woods	shack	river

Activity 3: A Log of Statehood

Teacher Note: This project has been done using *ClarisWorks*. Any database program can be used, if properly modified.

Students create a database to chronologically order the states as they entered the Union.

Background Knowledge: Manifest Destiny, statehood, reference skills, chronological order

Step 1: Determine the Dates of Statehood

Lead a discussion about Manifest Destiny. (*This was the belief that expanding to its natural borders was the destiny of the United States.*) Ask your students to guess how many years had passed between the date the first colony became a state and the date the fiftieth state entered the Union. Which do they think was the first state? the last? Record your students' guesses on the board. Have your students use almanacs to discover the dates each of the 50 states entered the Union. (You may wish to divide this task among five groups, each group researching ten states.) Have your students record their data on charts and post them at the front of the classroom. As a class, chronologically list each state as it entered the Union. Then have your students create a database of this information to use as a study guide or to refer to while further researching the 50 states.

Step 2: Create a Database

1. Upon launching *ClarisWorks*, click **Database**. Click **OK**. The dialog box that appears allows you to enter the categories (called fields) you will need to create your database. Type in the name (or title) of the first field, probably "State." Click **Create**. Type in the name of the second field name, "Date," and click **Create** again. For right now, you will only be creating these two fields to enter your data. Click **Done**.

2. The field names will appear with text boxes. In the text box next to the field name "State," type in the name of the first state that entered the Union (Delaware). Click on the text box next to the field name "Date" (or depress the Tab key) to move to the next field. Type in the date the state entered the Union (December 7, 1787).

3. To create duplicate fields, select **Edit...New Record**. Continue entering data and creating new records until all 50 states are entered chronologically in the database file.

Activity 3: A Log of Statehood *(cont.)*

Students may wish to experiment with the various ways to organize and sort their data. For example, they can organize their data in spreadsheet fashion by selecting **Layout...List**. They can rearrange their data so that the states are listed alphabetically by selecting **Organize...Sort Records**. Click on the field name "State" from the "Field List" and then click **Move**. This category will appear under the heading "Sort Order." Select **Ascending order** to view the states in alphabetical order from *A* to *W* or **Descending order** to view from *W* to *A*. Click **OK**. To change back to chronological order, move the "State" field name back under the "Field Name" heading and move "Date" to the "Sort Order" box. Choose **Ascending order** and click **OK**. The states will reappear in chronological order in the document.

Example: Database entries with two fields: "State" and "Date"

	Database (DB)
State	Vermont
Date	March 4, 1791
State	Kentucky
Date	June 1, 1792
State	Tennessee
Date	June 1, 1796
State	Ohio
Date	March 1, 1803
State	Louisana
Date	April 30, 1812
State	Indiana
Date	December 11, 1816
State	Mississippi
Date	December 10, 1817

Records: 11
Unsorted

Activity 3: A Log of Statehood *(cont.)*

Step 3: Finish and Print

Have your students edit their data and then save their databases to their disks for later use or print them to use as study guides. Have your students use their databases to answer the two questions posed at the beginning of the lesson. Then have them generate their own trivia questions to ask the class.

Example:

- What was the greatest length of time between two states' entries to the Union?
- Which states were admitted in the twentieth century?
- Which two states share the same entry date?

Chronological Order of States Admitted to the Union			
1. Delaware	12/07/1787	26. Michigan	01/26/1837
2. Pennsylvania	12/12/1787	27. Florida	03/03/1845
3. New Jersey	12/18/1787	28. Texas	12/29/1845
4. Georgia	01/02/1788	29. Iowa	12/28/1846
5. Connecticut	01/09/1788	30. Wisconsin	05/29/1848
6. Massachusetts	02/06/1788	31. California	09/09/1850
7. Maryland	04/28/1788	32. Minnesota	05/11/1858
8. South Carolina	05/23/1788	33. Oregon	02/14/1859
9. New Hampshire	06/21/1788	34. Kansas	01/29/1861
10. Virginia	06/25/1788	35. West Virginia	06/20/1863
11. New York	07/26/1788	36. Nevada	10/31/1864
12. North Carolina	11/21/1789	37. Nebraska	03/01/1867
13. Rhode Island	05/29/1790	38. Colorado	08/01/1876
14. Vermont	03/04/1791	39. North Dakota	11/02/1889
15. Kentucky	06/01/1792	40. South Dakota	11/02/1889
16. Tennessee	06/01/1796	41. Montana	11/08/1889
17. Ohio	03/01/1803	42. Washington	11/11/1889
18. Louisiana	04/30/1812	43. Idaho	07/03/1890
19. Indiana	12/11/1816	44. Wyoming	07/10/1890
20. Mississippi	12/10/1817	45. Utah	01/04/1896
21. Illinois	12/13/1818	46. Oklahoma	11/16/1907
22. Alabama	12/14/1819	47. New Mexico	01/06/1912
23. Maine	03/15/1820	48. Arizona	02/14/1912
24. Missouri	08/10/1821	49. Alaska	01/03/1959
25. Arkansas	06/15/1836	50. Hawaii	08/21/1959

Activity 4: Graphing States' Land Areas

Teacher Note: This project has been done using *ClarisWorks*. Any spreadsheet program can be used, if properly modified.

Students compare six states' land areas west of the Mississippi River to six states' land areas east of the Mississippi River, create a bar graph of the data, and write a summary report of their findings.

Background Knowledge: reference skills, the contour of the United States around 1800, the 50 states

Step 1: Research the States

After entering the years states entered the Union in a database (see Activity 3), students can compare their areas. Display a map featuring the territorial growth of the United States. (See page 9.) Also display a current United States map so that students may compare the area of land owned by our country as of 1783 to the expanse of land yet to be assimilated. What do they notice about the states that entered the union after borders were assigned to the original thirteen colonies? (*They seem to cover a greater area; they become more square.*) Why do they think that might be? (*The Ordinance of 1785 proclaimed that the land west of the colonies (the Old Northwest) would be divided into townships, an area of land covering thirty-six square miles. The townships were divided into 36 sections, each covering one square mile (640 acres). Each section could then be divided into smaller sections. Settlers could purchase a whole section for one dollar per acre ($640). Land north of the Ohio River became the Northwest Territory per the Northwest Ordinance of 1787. This ordinance also allowed this territorial land to enter the Union as states provided that it was divided into no more than five and no fewer than three states. Because of the townships, the states took on a more square appearance than the original thirteen colonies.*) Have your students continue their observations of the states west of the Mississippi River. (*They appear to become even larger and more square.*)

Have your students select six states west of the Mississippi River and six east of the Mississippi river to compare land areas. The students use almanacs to research the approximate area of six states that were formed from the Louisiana Purchase and points westward, as well as six states formed from the land owned by the United States as of 1783. You may wish to have students find the average land area for both sets of data.

Taking technology one step further . . . Logging this information into an existing database

Students can log this information into the database they created in Activity 3 if they desire. After opening the database file, select **Layout...Define Fields**. Type in the name of the next field (perhaps "Area"), and click **Create**, then click **Done**. Notice that the new field name appears with every record. Students need only type in the information for the states they have researched.

Step 2: Create a Spreadsheet

Now that students have their data in hand, they log it into a spreadsheet file and create a graph.

1. Launch *ClarisWorks* and click on **Spreadsheet**. Click **OK**.

Activity 4: Graphing States' Land Areas *(cont.)*

2. Students will create three categories of information along row one, beginning in column B. Type "Land East of the Mississippi River" in cell B1, "Land West of the Mississippi River" in cell C1, and "Average" in cell D1 (if applicable). Have them type the names of the six states east of the Mississippi River down column A, skip two spaces, and then type the names of the six states west of the Mississippi River in the same column. They may then input the area for the first six states in column B and the second six states in column C. The average for the first six states will be input in cell D8 and for the second states in cell D16.

Hint: Type in only the states' abbreviations so that they don't appear overcrowded in the chart.

3. Have your students save this file and name it accordingly.

Sample Spreadsheet

	A	B	C	D	E	F
				States' Land Areas (SS)		
B1	×✓	Land East of the Mississippi River				
1		Land East of the	Land West of the	Average		
2	DE	2489				
3	NJ	8722				
4	MA	10555				
5	SC	32007				
6	RI	1545				
7	FL	65756				
8				20179		
9						
10	CO		104100			
11	NV		110567			
12	NE		77358			
13	WY		104100			
14	UT		84904			
15	AZ		114006			
16				99173		
17						
18						

Activity 4: Graphing States' Land Areas *(cont.)*

Step 3: Create a Graph

Next your students use this data to create a graph.

1. Click and drag to highlight the data you want included in your chart, including words and numbers.

2. Click on **Options...Make Chart**. Decide on the most suitable chart for your needs (probably a bar graph) and click on it.

3. Select Labels from the "Modify" box to the left. Here you have the option of titling your chart. Decide where you want the title and legend to appear in relation to the graph by clicking the open circles to the far right. Click **OK**. If you will be printing in black and white only, be sure the "Color" option is not selected. Click **OK**. The chart will appear over the spreadsheet.

Step 4: Write a Summary Report

Have your students write a summary report explaining the comparative data in the word processing application of *ClarisWorks*. They should head the paper with a title and include their names on their reports. When they are done typing, have them save the file and then import their graphs to accompany the reports.

Taking technology one step further . . . Creating a headline in Drawing

Students can create headlines for their reports in the drawing application of *ClarisWorks*. Rather than simply adjusting the size of the text in the headline, students can also create decorative borders around their titles.

To import a headline using Drawing:

1. From the open word processing file, choose **File...New**. Select **Drawing** and then click **OK**. This will open a drawing page on top of your word processing page.

2. From the toolbox, select one of the space items (rectangle, oval, rounded-corner rectangle, etc.). Click and drag a box the approximate size you desire. A word of caution . . . don't make this box too long, or it may not fit in your word processing document.

3. From the toolbox, select the capital "A." This is the typing tool. You will need to create a text field before you begin typing. Click and drag over the box to create a text field. Use the task bar similar to that of word processing to adjust text size, style, alignment, font, etc. Type your headline. Then click outside the text field.

Activity 4: Graphing States' Land Areas *(cont.)*

4. Group the box and text field to make it one graphic item by holding down the shift key and clicking on the box and again on the text field. You will see a set of four dark squares on the outside corners of each field (eight in all—four around the box, four around the text field). Click and drag on **Arrange...Group**. The eight dark squares will change to four around the entire field.

5. Go to **Edit** and drag down to **Copy**. Then close this window (**File...Close**). You will want to save the changes and name the summary report something other than the title of the word processing document in case you need to go back and make any changes in it.

6. Place the cursor where you want your headline. Import it into your word processing document by choosing **Edit...Paste**. If you need to resize it, click on it once. This will highlight the item. Click and drag the dark square in the bottom right corner to resize it.

Step 5: Import the Graph to Word Processing

1. From the open word processing document, select **File...Open**. Select the name of the file with the spreadsheet and graph and then click **Open**. Make sure the graph is highlighted with a dark square at each corner. Select **Edit...Copy**.

2. Diminish the size of the spreadsheet file by clicking and dragging on the bottom right corner. The word processing document will appear beneath it. Click on it to bring it to the front.

3. Place the cursor where you wish the graph to appear, then select **Edit...Paste**. The graph will appear where the cursor had been. If it needs resizing, click on the graph. Tiny shadowed lines will appear around the outside edges. Click the bottom right corner of the chart and drag it across or down to resize it as needed.

Step 6: Finish and Print

Carefully edit the word processing document. Be careful not to accidentally delete the graph. You may wish to save the word processing file immediately after you import the graph. If you do delete the graph, immediately select **Edit...Undo Delete**. The chart will reappear at once. Print your students' reports. Have them give a brief oral report explaining their findings.

Desktop Publishing: An Introduction

Many times the need arises for more than just a word processing program. Desktop publishing offers the computer user alternative formats for items such as cards, banners, brochures, newsletters, and documents with borders and visual niceties.

One very child-oriented program is *Creative Writer*, which is discussed and used in the following pages. Other desktop publishing programs include *Print Shop* and *SuperPrint*. A person with general word processing skills should have no trouble adjusting to desktop publishing programs, since these programs are very similar to word processing programs. Their added benefit is you can be more creative with the projects you do. For example, in the activity "WANTED: DEAD OR ALIVE!" you are given the opportunity to create a poster combining text, art, and graphics in the same document.

Welcome to "Imaginopolis!" *Creative Writer* is a word processing program with several special features allowing students to be creative when working on their projects. In addition to applying basic word processing skills, *Creative Writer* offers students the opportunity to produce cards, banners, newspapers, and documents with borders. It also has a story starter application and unique text and audio features. If your school does not have *Creative Writer*, you can still complete the activities described in this book with similar desktop publishing programs such as *Print Shop* or *SuperPrint*. If your school does utilize *Creative Writer*, get acquainted with this program in "*Creative Writer* Basics." Then let your students' imaginations run wild!

Creative Writer Basics

This is a brief guide through the features in *Creative Writer*. This program can be tricky for first-time users. So follow the instructions carefully to have a successful experience with this outstanding creative writing program.

Getting into "Imaginopolis"

When you first begin this program, you will be asked to sign in. If you are saving to disk, click the down arrow until you see the title of your disk and then click on it. You can click **I'm New** and follow the directions if this is your first visit to *Creative Writer*. But if you use a different computer the next time you log in, your name will not be there. You can also log in under someone else's name.

If you sign in under a new name, be sure to insert your disk and tell the computer to save your work there. Then "go straight to Imaginopolis." Click the "Enter" door. Then click the revolving door. You will "want to start writing on (your) own." The computer will tell you to click the second story to go to the "**Writing Studio**." This is where you create regular word processing documents.

Desktop Publishing: An Introduction *(cont.)*

Creative Writer Basics *(cont.)*

In the Writing Studio

To use this program effectively, follow the procedures in the order listed below. When beginning, click **Write something new**. (You will need to double-click the blank page.)

Backgrounds: Find the book with the ruler icon in the task bar and click. Then click on **Background**. Select a background you like and then click anywhere on the page.

Borders: Follow the directions to choose a background and then click the slot machine arm. There are three sets of borders to choose from. Select a border that appeals to you and click anywhere on the page.

Text: Click on the large capital "A" in the task bar. You will see the typing tools, and a cursor will appear on the blank page. Begin typing your document, regardless of font or size. It is easier to go back and change the text after you are done typing.

Editing Text: Select the appropriate typing tools to change your text. For example, the one on the far left will change the font. When you have selected a font you want, the cursor will change to a paintbrush. Click and drag the paintbrush to highlight all the text you want in that font. You can also change the size, color, style, and alignment in this manner.

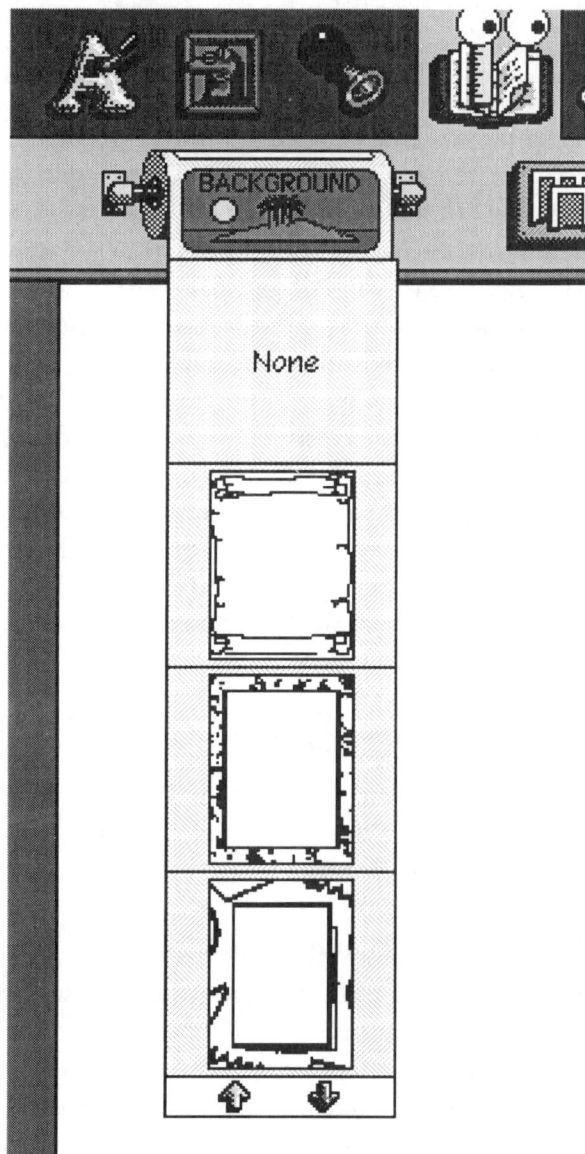

If you have time to "play," try clicking the slot machine arm while in the typing prompt to experience a host of unique text effects.

To check document spelling, click the bee in the task bar. *Creative Writer* will notify you of any spelling errors you may have made.

Desktop Publishing: An Introduction *(cont.)*

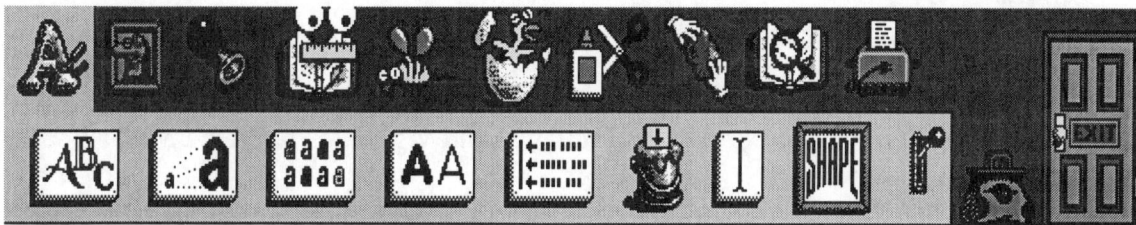

Creative Writer **Basics** *(cont.)*

Graphics: Next to the typing icon is the "sticker" icon. Click this. Use the up and down arrows to view a variety of graphics you can import into your document. Once you choose a sticker, your cursor will change to a pointer. Point to the location you want your graphic and click. By clicking and dragging the grabbing hand, you can move the graphic where you like it. Click outside the graphic to return to typing.

Editing Graphics: To change the size of the graphic, select the hands squishing gooey stuff from the task bar (third from the right). Select the appropriate tool from this menu to adjust the size of your graphic.

You can also color your pictures by double-clicking on them. Use the paint tools to assign colors to the pictures.

Printing: Click the toaster popping up a piece of paper. Select the printer icon on the left for a "fast print." Then click **Next**. Be patient! The background, border, and/or graphic images take up a lot of memory, and your printer may need time to "read" all the information. When the snake has slithered all the way across the screen, click **Stop**.

Exit: Click the **EXIT** door and follow the directions.

Editing Tip: #1: If you make a mistake, immediately choose the hatching egg. This will allow you to undo your error, but it will only undo the last thing you did, sequentially and in reverse. (If you wish to undo something you did three moves ago, you will first have to undo the most recent two changes.) A word of advice . . . complete the text portion of your document before adding any graphics. The only way to remove graphic images is to click the hatching egg and undo them.

Editing Tip: #2: Anytime you are having difficulty, read the help balloons from the guy in the carpetbag next to the exit door. This is McZee. He will help you through any difficulties you may have. If he is not there, click on the carpetbag and then on the goofy face. If you want to get rid of him, do the same.

Troubleshooting: Often a font you choose may not be installed in the printer. When this happens, your file will not print. You can try printing on a different computer. If this does not work, you may have to go back and change the font in your document.

Activity 5: WANTED: DEAD OR ALIVE!

Teacher Note: This project has been done using *Creative Writer*. Any desktop publishing program can be used, if properly modified.

Students use their knowledge of frontier bandits, outlaws, and vigilantes to create a "Wanted" poster of a fictitious or real-life outlaw.

Background Knowledge: outlaw raids, vigilante groups, research skills

Step 1: The "Old West"

Lead a discussion about the dangers posed by outlaws and bandits for settlers and travelers in the West. (*Gangs raided towns, pillaged, plundered, attacked, fought, and generally did anything they had a mind to.*) Since little was done to establish honest law and order, citizens from San Francisco formed their own method of law in a Vigilante Committee in 1851. Prominent business owners decided the fates of 89 outlaws, usually with brief trials and strict punishments. Although this Vigilante Committee only lasted 100 days, soon towns across the West were forming their own Vigilante groups to deal with local lawlessness.

Step 2: The Outlaws

Ask your students to brainstorm a list of the more popularly known outlaws. Complete the list, using the examples from page 25. Have each student research a chosen outlaw or discover an additional lawbreaker to research. When they are ready to create their "Wanted" posters, they may either use the names of the outlaws they researched or create fictitious bandits and use their research as background information.

Step 3: Create a WANTED Poster

Have your students create "Wanted" posters for their criminals in the "Writing Studio" of *Creative Writer*. They should include as much information as possible about their bandits' wrong-doings, where they may be found, and any other pertinent information which may help law abiding citizens discover the outlaws whereabouts.

Activity 5: WANTED: DEAD OR ALIVE! *(cont.)*

Step 4: Finish and Print

Help your students edit their posters for spelling errors, content, or unaligned words. Then have them print their final posters on parchment paper, if possible. Post them in the hall under the heading "WANTED FROM THE OLD WEST."

Famous Outlaws from the Old West

- Sam Bass
- Roy Bean
- Dianne "Gunslinger" Kelly
- Billy the Kid
- Butch Cassidy and the Sundance Kid (The "Wild Bunch")
- The Dalton Brothers
- Jesse James (The James Brothers)
- Bat Masterson
- Joaquin Murieta
- Belle Starr
- James Younger (The Younger Brothers)

Joaquin Murieta was the name given to a famous Mexican bandit who lived during the gold rush years of the 1800s. He became a hero of all Spanish-speaking people for encouraging them to resist working in the gold fields because of a monthly $20 tax imposed on foreign miners. No one is really sure if Joaquin Murieta really existed. As many as five bandits known as Joaquin roamed the gold fields during the 1850s. In 1853, lawmen killed two Mexicans and later identified one as Joaquin Murieta. The story of Joaquin Murieta has become so believable because of stories written by several respected writers.

Activity 5: WANTED: DEAD OR ALIVE! *(cont.)*

WANTED
DEAD OR ALIVE !

JOAQUIN MURIETA
**Believed to be the Leader of the Mexican Raiders
Protesting the Anti-Mexican Laws
Wanted for Robbing Stagecoach Riders and Miners
Last Seen in the Sacramento Valley**

REWARD $5,000

Activity 6: A Tall Tale

Teacher Note: This project has been done using *Creative Writer*. Any desktop publishing program can be used, if properly modified.

Students use what they know about tall tales to create a legend about a historical landmark (such as Pike's Peak) to explain how it got its name.

Background Knowledge: map reading, legends and myths

Step 1: Think and Plan

Build your students' knowledge of historical sites, towns, roads, or landmarks named after real-life people in your area. Explain that many landmarks and towns are so named because of the explorers and settlers who traveled there. Some may have achieved a great accomplishment; others may have been the first to explore the region and so the town was named after them.

Have your students view a map or atlas of the United States and point out landmarks, towns, or points of interest that may have been named after someone famous. Decide on one location as a class. Have your students work together to write a legend or myth describing how that town got its name. The wilder the story, the better. Then have your students work in teams of two or three to select a location in the West from the map to write an original legend or myth explaining how that town got its name.

Step 2: Create a Story in *Creative Writer*

Have your students use their ideas to write a myth or legend in *Creative Writer*. You may wish to have your students write their stories on paper first and then type it in, using a computer. This assignment is meant to be a creative writing project. Students may print their stories when they are done, but they will share them from the computer to take advantage of the text and audio features available to make their stories more complete.

Have your students decide on a background or border. Then they type and edit their stories and add graphics. Once your students have finished, they may embellish their projects with unique text and audio features.

(Remember, McZee will help you if you have any questions. Click the carpetbag, then McZee, and then the feature you are unsure of. He really is a big help. Also, if you try something you don't like, be sure to click the hatching egg and **Undo** immediately.)

Shape Words Click the "Shape" box in the task bar while in the typing prompt to create a shape for the title of your story. Experiment with various shapes, fonts, colors, and patterns until you are satisfied.

Text: Click the slot machine arm while in the typing prompt. Try boxing words in different colors or select one of the "special," "combo," or fancy letters options.

Activity 6: A Tall Tale *(cont.)*

Sound:

Have a word or picture in mind you wish to attach a sound to. Click the horn along the top of the task bar. Select a sound and then click on the word or picture to attach it. Graphics will remain the same, but a box will appear around words that will play a sound. When you are ready to share your story, click on the carpetbag, and then on the magic wand. Clicking on the items with sound by using the wand will activate the audio feature.

Step 3: Finish and Share

Help your students edit their stories one final time before they share them. They may print their stories if they wish. Some of the textual features will print; others will not. Decide how you wish to have your students share their stories. You may wish to have a few students share each day during oral reading time after recess. Or your students can share their stories with their "reading buddies" from a lower grade. Another option is to have your students choose adults on staff with whom they would like to share and arrange a convenient time for those persons to visit with the students. If you invite parents to join in a "Wild West Show," you can have your students share their stories with their parents.

Multimedia Presentations: An Introduction

Text documents are all well and good, but to capture the attention of today's students, one often must reach far beyond what word processing or desktop publishing has to offer. Enter multimedia programs—software that implements the multiple use of media (e.g., text, films, audio, graphics, animation, etc.). *HyperStudio* is probably the most widely used and recognized multimedia program found in schools today. Whether your school uses this or a different multimedia program, students will have the ability to import graphics, sound, animation, and video to accompany their text documents.

The use of these interactive programs results in the completion of astounding projects, the fostering of a tremendous sense of pride by students in their work, and the learning of valuable computer skills. Every student should be fortunate enough to have successfully completed a multimedia project during his/her academic life.

Nearly all of us have experienced the awkwardness of having to stand in front of a large number of people to give a speech or report for the first time. We stand before our peers, frantically flipping through our note cards, desperately trying to maintain eye contact with our audience, and miserably failing to sound interesting. Of course, everyone understands our situation, tries to act interested in what we are saying, and politely applauds when we are through. Then, for the rest of the day, we feel incredibly self-conscious and paranoid about what our friends may be saying to each other about that dreadful speech we made. Of course, nothing could be farther from the truth. The fact is, no one really cared about our speech; they are glad it wasn't them up there making fools of themselves, and they never gave our speech a second thought. All the same, it was a miserable experience we fervently hoped we never had to do again.

Is it really possible that a computer program can change all that? No, actually, it isn't. But *HyperStudio* can perk up the monotony of giving a speech. Speeches are usually more interesting when we use visual aids. *HyperStudio* provides plenty of those. Speeches become compelling when accompanied by a movie, video, slide presentation, or dramatic display. *HyperStudio* in itself is a slide show. Users can incorporate sounds, animation, or laserdisc features to further enhance their reports. One can also provide background music to hold an audience's attention. The possibilities when creating a report with *HyperStudio* are nearly limitless.

The *HyperStudio* pages (or cards) take the place of the note cards you would otherwise use when giving a speech. "Buttons" connect the cards so the report flows smoothly from one idea to the next. "Text boxes" are imported so that you may type the words that make up the actual report. You can import graphics (or simple pictures) to supplement the text. From this point on, the use of multimedia functions is what makes your report so grand. The button is the tool used to include sounds, animation, video graphics, and/or a myriad of additional multimedia features.

Multimedia Presentations: An Introduction *(cont.)*

Creating a report has never been more involved nor more exciting. Of course, students will still need to give their speeches, but with the help of this powerful multimedia program, their speeches will invite their audiences to share in their presentations, not act as mere sounding boards for words and pictures.

All of the *HyperStudio* functions you need to know to create a basic multimedia project are described in "*HyperStudio* Basics." Refer to this section of the book if you need assistance regarding the directions in the activities described in "*HyperStudio* Activities."

HyperStudio Basics

New Stack

The first step when beginning a project is to prepare your cards. From the *HyperStudio* home page, click **New Stack**. When starting a new stack, you will notice that the first card is untitled. Before adding anything to your stack, go to **File...Save Stack**. Here you can decide the name you wish to give your stack (probably the title of the topic you are working on) and tell the computer where you want this stack saved. The computer will only open one card in your new stack. To make new cards, click on **Edit** and drag down to **New Card**. Continue to make new cards until you have the proper number you had planned for this stack.

If the first card does not read "Card 1" after the title, choose **Edit...Preferences**. Click on the box that reads "Show card number with stack name." This will allow you to keep track of the multitude of cards you will be creating so that you can organize them in the stack more easily. Then click **OK**.

You will need to use the toolbox for a variety of functions. Take your cursor up to **Tools**. Click and drag all the way past the bottom of the toolbox. You will see a dotted outline appear on the screen. Release the mouse. The toolbox will remain on the screen until you decide you don't need it anymore. To get rid of it, click on the open square in the upper left corner of the toolbox. If you need to move it to a different location on the card while you are working, click the dotted area along the top of the toolbox and drag it to the spot you wish to move the tools.

Use the finger (or pointer) to make your actions active. Use the arrow (or edit tool) when you need to edit or move a particular item. The other tools in the toolbox are shortcuts to various functions not described in this manual. Notice that the painting and drawing tools are below the function tools. Practice using each of these if you are unfamiliar with their functions.

You will also probably want to use varying colors as well. You can ready your color box by clicking and dragging on **Colors** in the same manner you did for the toolbox.

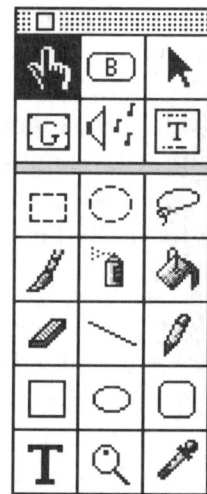

Backgrounds

Every card you create in a stack should have a background. Before you begin working, decide on a background you like for each card. Click on **File...Import Background**. Choose from one of the many graphics available in the "HS Art" file. Then click **Open**. The background you selected will appear on your card.

Multimedia Presentations: An Introduction *(cont.)*

HyperStudio Basics *(cont.)*

You may also choose to simply fill in your card with a different color. Choose a color you like and then click the paint can icon in the toolbox. Click anywhere on your card. The can will fill the card with the color you chose.

You can also change the colors in an imported background, using the painting tools and color box. Experiment with the painting functions until you are satisfied with your background.

Text Fields

In order to type your text, you will first have to create a text box. Click on **Objects...Add a Text Object**. Click and drag the four-arrow cursor to place your text box where you want it. You can move the cursor to either edge or the top or bottom of the text box and click and drag the two-arrow cursor to change the dimensions of the box. When the box is the size you desire, click anywhere on the outside of the box. An options dialog box will appear. Choose a text and background color. Decide if you want the scroll bar to show a scrollable text and the frame drawn. The "Read only" option allows you to "lock" your text field so that no one can make changes to the text you have written. Choose the **Style** option to change the font, size, and style of the letters, as well as their alignment. Click **OK**. You should see a blinking cursor in your text box. This indicates that you may begin typing.

Graphics

To add pictures, click on **Objects...Add a Graphic Object**. Choose one of the picture pages from the HS Art menu. Click **Open**. If you want a boxed graphic, choose the dotted box icon in the top left corner. You may also wish to choose only a picture without the background color or may need to maneuver around other pictures. In this case, choose the lasso icon located next to the dotted box icon. Click and drag a field around the picture you want. Then click **OK**. Remember, everything within the red marching ants will be imported onto your card. Click and drag the picture to its designated place on the card. Click outside the picture. The options in the dialog box that appears allow you to decide to draw a frame around your picture and/or give it an action (see "Actions"). Then click **OK**.

Buttons

Buttons provide the actions you want to make your project more interesting. They allow you to move from one card to the next or add a sound, animation, video, or other presentation function. These same actions can be devised using graphics (above), but you can type direction clues on the buttons (e.g., next, back, home, try this, etc.). All the cards in your stack should be nearly complete so you can properly identify where each button will take you and/or what it will do.

HyperStudio Basics *(cont.)*

To create a button, click **Objects...Add a Button**. Type the directions in the box that says "Name:." These words will appear in the button. Decide on name (text) and background colors for your button and choose the type or style of outline you prefer. You can give your button a little more pizazz by adding an icon. When you are all through here, click **OK**. Click and drag the button to where you want to place it on the page. Click anywhere outside the button. Use the options in the dialog box that appears to decide on a place for the button to go and/or a thing for it to do (see "Actions"). If you don't have a place for it to go, leave this as **None of the above** until you have all your cards in place. You can always go back and edit the button later (see "Editing Tips").

Unless you know all your cards will be completed in sequential order, do not choose the **Next card**, **Previous card**, or **Back** options. If your cards somehow get out of order, you will then need to go back and edit all the buttons on all the cards. Your best option is to choose **Another card** and assign the number of the card to which this button should move.

Once you have told this button *where* to go, a transitions dialog box will appear. Now you need to decide *how* you want your button to move from one card to the next. Try changing the speed and manner of transition and then click **Try it**. The computer will demonstrate how your card will change from one to the next. When you have completed making your selections, click **OK**.

Actions

There are many actions to choose from in the **Things to Do** box. The directions for each option are clearly stated as you progress from beginning to end. Buttons can do many things at one time. Try assigning your button to move to the next card while simultaneously playing a sound.

Editing Tips

This can be a complicated program for people who are unfamiliar with its applications. If you inadvertently make a mistake, fix it right away. Click on **Edit...Undo**, and the computer will reverse the last change you made to your card. But remember, you can only edit the last thing you did. Trying this again will only undo what you just undid (or put it back the way it was before you undid it).

If you are unhappy with a button, text box, or graphic, choose the arrow from the toolbox and click on the item you wish to change. The red marching ants will appear around this item. Then click on **Edit** and drag down to **Edit This** (**Button**, **Text**, **Graphic**). The options window will reappear and allow you to make any changes you feel are necessary.

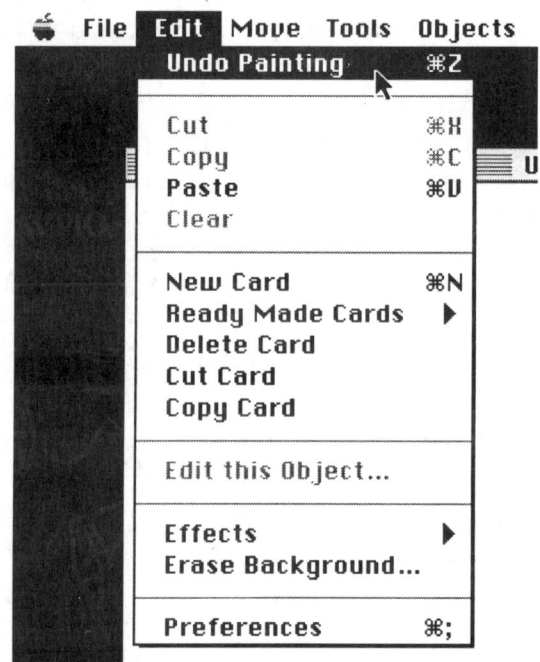

HyperStudio Basics *(cont.)*

If you need to edit the actual text you typed, simply choose the pointing finger from the toolbox. As you move your cursor from the card to the text field, the pointer will change to a typing cursor. Click where you want to edit your text and edit away. To change a text style, use the cursor to highlight the text you wish to change and choose **Options...Text Style**. Using the arrow to get the marching ants will only edit the text object or box (to give it an action, for example).

You can delete whole text fields, buttons, or graphics by choosing the arrow from the toolbox and clicking on the item you wish to delete. Then push the delete key on the keyboard. The item you selected will disappear. Oops! Wrong item? Remember to immediately use the **Edit...Undo** option to bring it back.

You may need to connect cards or stacks that have been stored on separate disks. If this is the case, copy all the stacks that have cards you wish to link onto the hard drive, each with a different file name. Create a new stack. Import buttons onto the card(s) that will take you to those stacks. (Assign "Places to Go" in the actions dialog box to that of **Another stack**.)

Before you make your presentation, edit your text fields and run through each button action. Check to be sure your cards are all in the right order and that all actions work effectively. You may also wish to remove the "Show card number with stack name" option (**Edit...Preferences**) before you give your presentation so the audience, depending on their maturity level, will not make a point to tell you your cards are out of order. You should also lock your stack so no one can change any information you have worked so hard to prepare. To do this, go to **Edit...Preferences**. Enter your stack password and click the box to assign the "Lock stack" option.

One last suggestion . . . if you "borrowed" pictures or videos from another source, remember to give credit where credit is due. Identify your references where the items occur in your document or create a new card just for this purpose. List the companies who own the copyrights to the images you used. This will give your students practice in listing resources and avoiding copyright violations. You can also use this opportunity to discuss the dangers of plagiarism.

Implementing Multimedia in the Classroom

When beginning a multimedia project, you may wish to follow the suggested sequential steps listed below. This will help organize your daily plans and help students complete a successful project.

Before beginning, you may wish to prepare a multimedia report of your own to share with the class. Begin by standing before the class (without the computer) and reading just the text portion of your report. Answer any questions your students may have about your topic and discuss how you could improve on your report. Then share the very same report you prepared, using a multimedia presentation program such as *HyperStudio*. Have your students share their thoughts about this report. Did they like it better? Why? Explain the difference between a written report and a multimedia presentation. (*Multimedia utilizes technology to incorporate sounds, graphics, and animation or video to add to the text.*) Explain that they will have the opportunity to write a similar report of their own, using a program such as *HyperStudio* to share with the class.

Step 1: Research

Lead a discussion about the topic at hand. Then instruct your students to spend time gathering information and resources to use in their multimedia report. Discuss the kinds of information your students should gather and how they should organize the information they find.

Step 2: Planning Cards

Distribute 5" x 8" (13 cm x 20 cm) note cards for them to use to plan. They will use their research and planning cards to organize the information they have gathered. They should include text boxes, buttons, and graphics they wish to include.

Step 3: Preparing Cards in *HyperStudio*

Introduce the *HyperStudio* computer program. Explain that this multimedia program can achieve almost anything your students can imagine. The cards they see will take the place of the note cards they would use if they were to give a traditional oral report. Demonstrate how to open a new stack, use the tool and color boxes, and create backgrounds. Allow your students time to "play" with the background graphics and painting and drawing tools to create backgrounds for their cards. The students will need to choose **Edit...New Card** each time they are ready to prepare a new card. Have them save their work to a disk or to the hard drive, depending on your needs.

Implementing Multimedia in the Classroom *(cont.)*

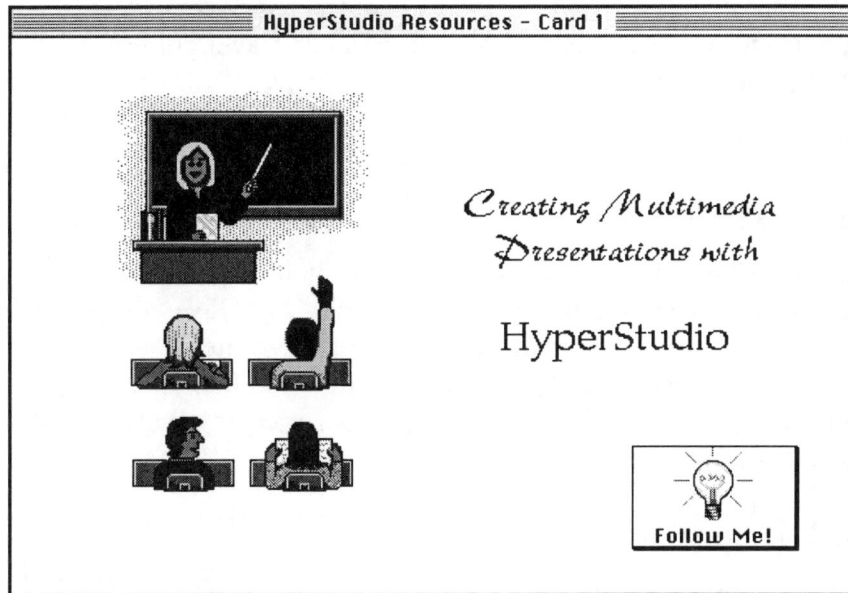

Step 4: Adding Text Fields

With their plans in hand, your students are ready to type their text on the cards. Demonstrate how to import a text object and prepare for typing. Your students should work on completing the text portion of their reports, including editing misspelled words, checking for punctuation errors, etc.

Step 5: Adding Graphics

Now that they have their text fields complete with their written reports, your students can import any graphic images they wish to display to accompany the text. Demonstrate this application. Then allow time for your students to place their graphic items on the appropriate pages.

Step 6: Adding Buttons

Once the cards are essentially complete with text and graphics, your students can work on linking their cards via buttons. They should tell each button where to go and/or what to do (see "*HyperStudio* Basics: Buttons"). When they have finished linking their cards appropriately, they should check to be sure that their button actions work correctly. If necessary, they can edit their buttons by selecting the arrow, clicking on the button, and choosing **Edit...Edit This Button**. By choosing "actions" from the dialog box that appears, they can make the necessary changes.

Step 7: Final Revisions

Your students should use this time to finish their projects and run through their productions at least once in preparation for their presentations. If your students finish early, they can use this opportunity to "play" with some "New Button Actions." Perhaps they will encounter unique multimedia applications which will make their presentations stand out from their classmates'.

Activity 7: Life in the West

Teacher Note: This project has been done using *HyperStudio*. Any multimedia program can be used, if properly modified.

Students use their knowledge of the western frontier to create a travel guide for other easterners who may be considering settling in the West.

Background Knowledge: Life as a Pioneer

Step 1: Thinking "West"

Use fictional and nonfictional accounts of western travels to help explain the hardships people endured traveling west (see "Additional Software Resources" on page 43). Have your students work in teams of between two and four to make three lists similar to the one below. In the first column, they brainstorm all the necessities a western traveler needed and then prioritize the list. Next the teams list the dangers and inconveniences of traveling to the West and suggestions for easing these hardships. Finally, they list all the positive aspects the West has to offer for new settlers.

Step 2: Plan and Organize

Once the teams' lists are complete, have your students plan and organize their information for their *HyperStudio* projects. Give each team the number of 5" x 8" (13 cm x 20 cm) note cards they think they will need to complete their projects. They should decide which information they wish to include on each card and plan text boxes accordingly. If they use more than one card, they should include buttons on their planning cards and tell where the buttons will go. They should also plan some artwork or graphics they will create on their cards.

Traveling West		
Supplies Needed	Perils	Benefits

Step 3: Work in *HyperStudio*

Have your students use their planning cards to complete their *HyperStudio* projects. Refer to "Implementing Multimedia in the Classroom" for a brief outline of the steps your students should follow to create their stacks. For a more detailed explanation, see "*HyperStudio* Basics." Your students may need to spend more than one class period working on their projects, depending on their familiarity with this program and the length of their reports. Have the teams save their stacks to their disks and name them appropriately.

Activity 7: Life in the West *(cont.)*

Step 4: Share Student Presentations

Once all the teams have finished their stacks, have them run through them one last time to be sure all the buttons and actions work appropriately. Gather your students around the computer or attach the computer to an overhead projector or TV monitor for easier viewing. As students make their presentations, have the audience fill out a student survey sheet below for each team that presents. Explain that they may only write positive comments. Collect the sheets and redistribute them to the students who made the *HyperStudio* presentation. Each student will have the benefit of enjoying everyone else's report and making a positive remark to pass along.

Student Survey Sheet

My name_____

Multimedia report by_____

This report was about_____

I especially liked _____

_____

_____

Something new I learned was _____

_____

_____

_____

An idea for improvement is _____

_____

_____

_____

Activity 8: Westward, Ho!

Teacher Note: This project has been done using *HyperStudio*. Any multimedia program can be used, if properly modified.

Students research and report on one of the many ways people traveled during the Westward Movement. Your students' stacks are then linked to create one class report.

Background Knowledge: modes of transportation in the 1800s, research skills

Step 1: Research

Assign small groups of students to research the various means of travel used by people who lived during the Westward Movement. Encourage students to use multimedia references to find information and pictures to use in their reports. Your students may use the research guide on page 42 to help them find and reference pertinent information. After your students have completed their research, have them write a report explaining their findings.

Traveling West:	Conestoga Wagon	Stagecoach	Steamboat
	Canal Boat	Flatboat	Train

Taking technology one-step further . . . saving images from programs for later use

Students can save images they may come across while researching computer reference programs. Then, while completing their *HyperStudio* projects, they can access these images and import them onto their pages. This is an alternative to simply copying and pasting images from one program into *HyperStudio* where the program you may be copying from must be present while working in *HyperStudio*.

To save images from a computer program, do the following:

1. Find an image you wish to use. Click on it to make it active. Go to **Edit...Copy**. Then exit the program you are in.

2. Open the *ClarisWorks* program. Choose **Drawing**. Once you have a blank drawing page, go to **Edit...Paste**. The image you copied will appear on your drawing page with four solid black squares, one at each corner. This means the graphic image is active.

3. Choose **File...Save as**. In the dialog box that appears, select the file at the top in which you wish to save this image (probably your disk, or perhaps a new folder). Give the image a name and then select the "Save As:" option. Right now it reads *ClarisWorks*. Click and drag this box to select **PICT**. Then click **Save**. *ClarisWorks* will save this image as a "PICT file" on your disk or in the folder you selected.

To learn how to import this graphic from your file to your *HyperStudio* report, see "Taking technology one step further" on page 39.

Activity 8: Westward, Ho! *(cont.)*

How to save as PICT (Step 3)

Note: You can follow this procedure utilizing a "Flash It" or "PICTify" program that may be installed on your computer. When using this feature, your image will be sent to a scrapbook. You can then copy and paste the image from the scrapbook into the Drawing program of *ClarisWorks* and subsequently save it to your disk as a "PICT file" in the same fashion.

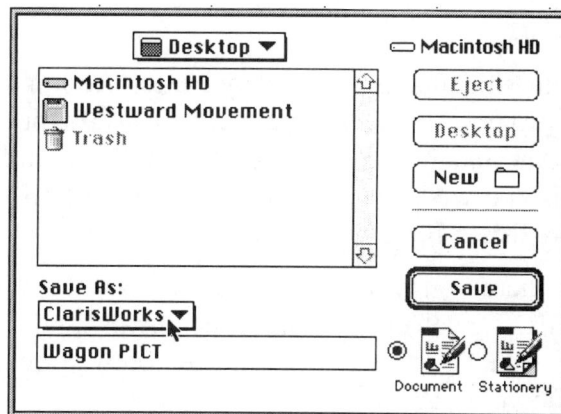

```
┌─────────────────────────────────────────┐
│   [▥ Desktop ▼]          ▭ Macintosh HD  │
│  ▭ Macintosh HD        ⇧   [  Eject  ]   │
│  ▥ Westward Movement       [ Desktop ]   │
│  🗑 Trash                   [ New  ☐ ]    │
│                            [ Cancel  ]   │
│                        ⇩   [  Save   ]   │
│  Save As:                                │
│  [ClarisWorks ▼]                         │
│  [Wagon PICT          ]  ◉ ▤  ○ ▤        │
│                          Document Stationery│
└─────────────────────────────────────────┘
```

Step 2: Work in *HyperStudio*

Students will essentially create three cards in their stacks: a title card, report card, and animation card. Allow the teams time to work on their first two cards. The title card should include a title, the students' names, and perhaps a brief introduction. A button should link to the next card. Card two is the report card. Students should import a text box to type their research reports. They may wish to include some artwork to dress up the text card or use some graphics they saved from another program, following the steps from "Importing graphics from saved files" on the following page. When they finish, be sure your students have saved their work and named their stacks appropriately.

Card three will be the animation card. Have students create their animations, perhaps using graphics from a multimedia reference program, following the explanation in "Animator" on the next page.

Taking technology one step further . . . utilizing additional *HyperStudio* features

Importing Graphics from Saved Files

To import graphics your students may have saved under another file name, select **Objects...Add a Graphic Object**. In the box under "Please select a picture file," choose the drive where the images are saved. Click **Open**. Select the image you want from this file and click **Open** again. Use the selection tools that appear in the top-left area of the screen to get your picture. Click and drag around as little or as much of the picture as you want to import. The graphic image you selected will be highlighted with red marching ants. Click **OK**. Click and drag the image to resize it and move it to the desired location on your card. If students are using the graphics they saved as part of their animation, do not have them import the graphics to their third cards, but rather follow the steps on the next page.

Activity 8: Westward, Ho! *(cont.)*

Animator

Have your students use this "New Button Action" to create animations of images they saved from another program. Select **Objects...Add a Button**. In the action dialog box that appears, choose **New Button Action**. In the "Names:" box in the next dialog box that appears, select **Animator**. Read the "Info:" if you wish to get an understanding of how to effectively use this "New Button Action." Then click **Use this NBA**.

Decide where you wish to retrieve the graphic. You can use one of the images you may have saved as a "PICT file" by selecting **From disk library** and then opening the appropriate file and graphic image. Select the image or part of the image you wish to animate. The part you selected will automatically appear on your card.

To animate WITHOUT CLICKING THE MOUSE, move the graphic where you wish to begin the animation. Then click and drag the image over your page. You will begin creating the animation the moment you click and drag the mouse. Adjust the features of your animation from the dialog box that appears after you release the mouse. Choose **Playback** to see what your animation will look like when you push the button. Click **OK** when done.

Step 3: Connect the Cards to Create One Report

Once all the teams are finished with their three-card stacks, transfer them (each with a different file name) to the hard drive. Begin a new stack. Create (or have teams of students create) a title and contents card. Create a button to link to each of the students' stacks. From the "Places to Go" section in the action dialog box that appears, select **Another stack**. Choose the team's stack to which this button will link. Click **Open**. Decide how you want it to go there and then click **Done**. Save this stack with a file name such as "Transportation in the West."

Once all the buttons are in place, select the pointing finger and try out each button to ensure that it links to the appropriate stack. While visiting the students' stacks, create a button on the third card to link back to the title and contents stack.

Step 4: Share the Class Report

Double-check the teams' graphic links to be sure they all work properly. Gather your students around the computer or attach the computer to an overhead projector or TV monitor for easier viewing. Share the project with your class and then invite another class to share your accomplishment.

Activity 8: Westward, Ho! *(cont.)*

Example: Activity 7: Student *HyperStudio* project about Conestoga wagons, card one (table of contents card).

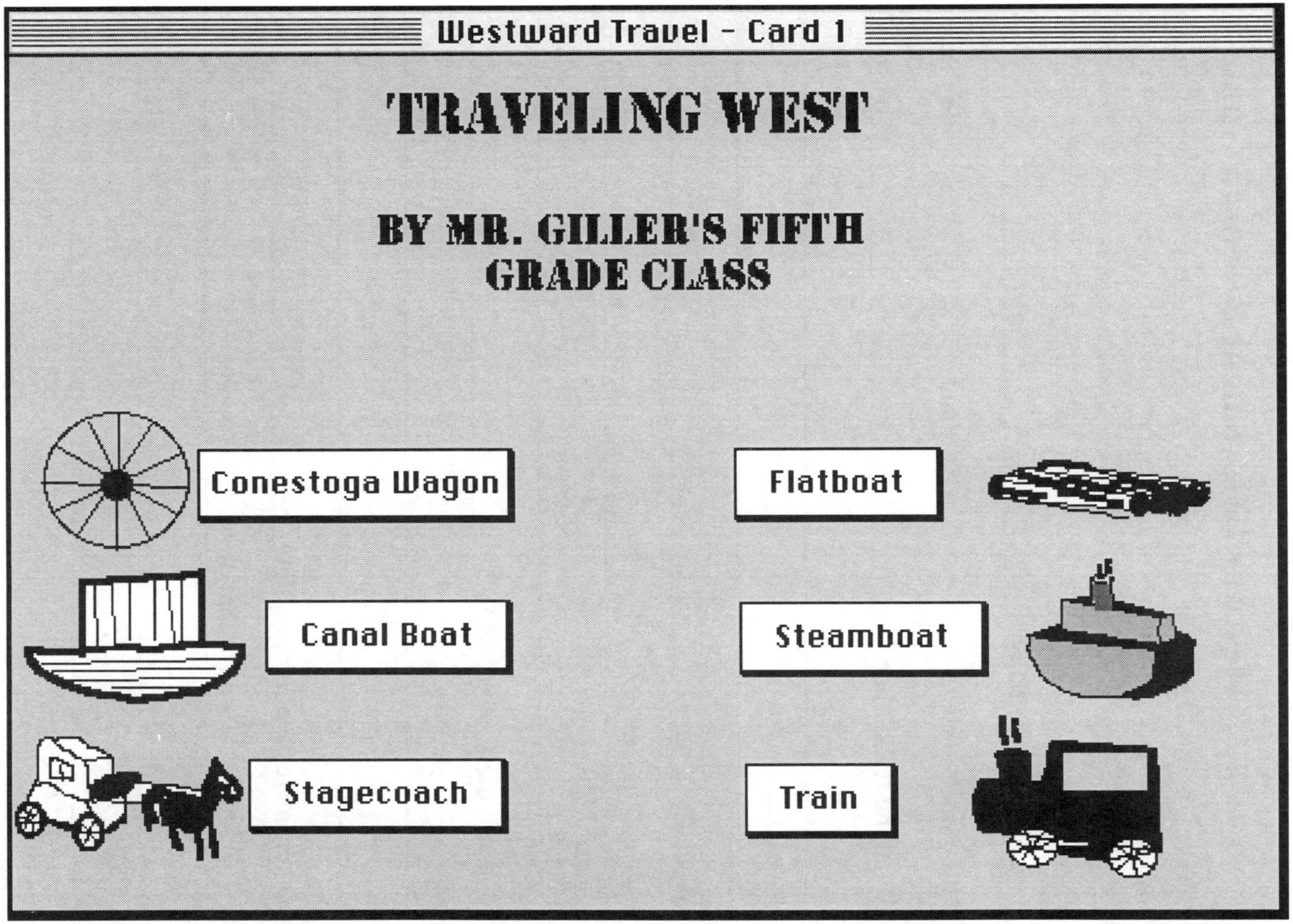

Westward Travel – Card 1

TRAVELING WEST

BY MR. GILEB'S FIFTH GRADE CLASS

Flatboat

Steamboat

Train

Conestoga Wagon

Canal Boat

Stagecoach

Activity 8: Westward, Ho! *(cont.)*

Names: _____

Westward Movement Research Guide

Directions: Use this sheet as a guide as you research a means of travel during the Westward Movement. Use additional paper, if necessary. Organize your information and record your resources on the back of this paper.

1. Mode of transportation _____

2. How was it used?   Over land   Over water   On rails

3. What did it look like? _____

   _____

   _____

4. What did it carry? _____

   _____

   _____

5. Is it still used today? How? _____

   _____

   _____

6. Other interesting information _____

   _____

   _____

   _____

   _____

7. On the back of this paper, draw a picture to show what it looked like.

Additional Software Resources

Software companies are quickly meeting the demands of advanced technology to fill a need in our schools. One can find multimedia and interactive software on just about any and every school-related subject, including science, social studies, reading, language, and math. Following is a highly motivating and interactive program you may wish to consider as part of your unit about the Westward Movement. Included also are a few activities you may wish to use to extend the program listed here.

Oregon Trail

This interactive, multimedia software is probably one of the most popular and widely used "games" to teach students about the hardships of life on "the Trail." Students decide on an occupation for the leader of the group and passengers who will be traveling with him or her. Then they are off to the general store to buy supplies and arrange transportation for their long journey. Along the way, students may visit strategic stopping points or landmarks to trade, chat with the locals, or rest. Throughout their travels, the computer keeps a log of important goings-on, explaining delays or remarking on deaths and illnesses.

- Although the goal of the game is to reach Oregon, many students get caught up in the excitement of the hunt, sometimes hunting without reason. Instruct your students to try their luck at hunting wild game only when food is running low. Many times they may kill far more buffalo or other animals than they can carry or pack away. Have your students write down how much food they waste each time they hunt. Use these totals as a means of teaching students about the decline of the American buffalo throughout the 1800s.

- Have your students take note of the delays and hardships travelers endured while traveling the trail. Read the story *Going West* by Jean Van Leeuwen. Students may then use their knowledge of westward travel and creative thinking skills to write an exciting tale about their journeys or the new lives they made for themselves out West. You may also wish to use this software and story as references when assigning activity seven: "Life in the West."

Writing Along The Oregon Trail

Looking for more creative ideas to use to make the *Oregon Trail* computer program more meaningful? This is a valuable resource you will want to use. This software provides you, the teacher, with suggested planning techniques and your students with bountiful realistic word processing activities to use in conjunction with the *Oregon Trail* (see above). Complete with teaching guide, *Writing Along The Oregon Trail* complements its already outstanding counterpart.

Exploring on the Internet

When considering instructional and research resources, try complementing your curriculum with information from Web sites on the Internet. The resources available to you on the Internet are virtually endless. One can find information, pictures, videos, and/or sound on nearly anything and everything. Your students will relish this unique opportunity to delve into the technological information age, expand their resource base, and search enthusiastically for related information.

Logging On

If you are unfamiliar with the Internet, elicit help from a co-worker to log onto your school's network and Web browser. The network is the phone line access you use to get to the Internet. A Web browser is the "viewer" you use to see what's out there. Access to the Internet may be a two-step process. You may need to first log onto a local network before hooking into a Web browser like *Netscape* or *Mosaic*. Others, like *America Online* and *CompuServ,* are networks and Web browsers all in one.

Finding Information

After you are safely logged onto a Web browser, you may begin searching for related topics and specific information. *Excite, Yahoo, Infoseek, Lycos,* and *Magellan* are popular search bases. By typing in a specific http://www.? (or uniform resource locator), you should be able to locate any Web site from any search base. You can also type in a subject of interest in the "search" box and click on **Search** to retrieve a host of related Web sites you may consider visiting.

A word of advice . . . the sites relating to Westward Expansion are few in number. Have a specific topic of interest ready to investigate. The more specific your topic, the easier your search will be. If you want to find information about Jesse James, type in his full name. If you are thinking of using the Internet as an instructional guide (to take a tour of the Oregon Trail, for example), spend some time investigating sites on the Internet before sharing them with your class to make sure the site you share is related to its purpose and does not hold any surprises for you. It is also easy to get lost once you start "surfing the 'Net." When you find a site that looks interesting, you can bookmark it by clicking the **Bookmark** prompt from the task bar at the top. Then, when you visit this Web site with your class, you need only find your bookmark from the list and click on it. The computer will take you right to that page.

Cool Web Sites

The Web sites listed here can be found by using any Internet service provider (e.g., *America Online*, *CompuServ*, *Prodigy*) or using a direct Internet access called Point to Point Protocol (PPP) through your school or a variety of services (e.g., *Earthlink*, *FlashNet*, etc.). Then you can view the Internet through *Netscape* and searching in *Yahoo*. Regardless of the network and Web browser your school uses, you should be able to search the database for the Web sites listed in this guide.

Keep in mind that Web sites tend to change over time. If these Web sites are no longer in existence, you can still find information by typing in a specific topic to search.

In Search of the Oregon Trail http://www.pbs.org/opb/oregontrail/

Get your students interested in more than just the computer game. This site has links to facts, myths, and trivia. There is also a teacher's guide which also lists facts about various points of interest related to this topic and suggests activities for students. Quiz your students' knowledge of "the Trail" by clicking on the trivia link.

The Great Gold Rush http://pwa.acusd.edu/~jross/goldrush.html

The Virtual California Gold Country http://www.malakoff.com/vcgc.htm

Want to learn more about the "fever" of the mid 1800s? Try either one of these valuable sites to help your students learn the facts behind the legends.

The Trail of Tears http://ngeorgia.com/history/nghisttt.shtml

Your students will always remember this compelling event in our nation's history upon visiting this site. Read a summary of the affair and link to related topics of interest.

WestWeb http://www.library.csi.cuny.edu/westweb/

WestWeb is a topically organized Web site about the study of the American West. Subjects include, *Children of the Sun, Empires of Expansion, Women Making it on Their Own, Where Men Were Men*, and many more!

The Autobiography of Calamity Jane http://www.cowgirls.com/dream/cowgals/calamity.htm

If your students are fascinated with outlaws of the Wild West, have them read up on one of America's most notorious gunslingers: Calamity Jane. Learn where and how she grew up and what prompted her to tempt fate.

The Internet and *HyperStudio*

For your more technologically advanced students, there is a way to import Web pages into a *HyperStudio* project. This is a fascinating way to include information in a multimedia report.

Finding a Web Page

First you must find an appropriate Web page that pertains to the report you are completing in *HyperStudio*. Log onto a network and "surf the 'Net" to find just the right Web site to accompany your report. Once you have what you are looking for, note the uniform resource locator or http://www.? site. You may wish to bookmark this page in case you need to find it later.

Working in *HyperStudio*

On the card you wish to import a Web page, add a button that will take you there. In the "Actions" dialog box, choose **New Button Action**. Under the "Names:" listing, arrow down until you find **NetPage** and click it. Read the "Info:" text box for more information about this new button action. When you are ready, click **Use this NBA**. Type in the "Uniform Resource Locator" (the http://www.? site) in the dialog box that appears. Then click **OK**. Click **OK** again from the "New Button Actions" dialog box. Then click **Done** from the "Actions" dialog box.

Before this button will work, your computer must be online and ready to transport the viewer to the Web page. Exit and save your *HyperStudio* stack. Log onto the network and Web browser you will be using. Go to **File...Close**. This will keep you online but close this window. On the far right of the task bar, find the Web browser icon. Click and drag it to select and view the "At Ease" screen. Open your *HyperStudio* file and stack. Find the card on which you imported the button to take you to the Web site and try it out.

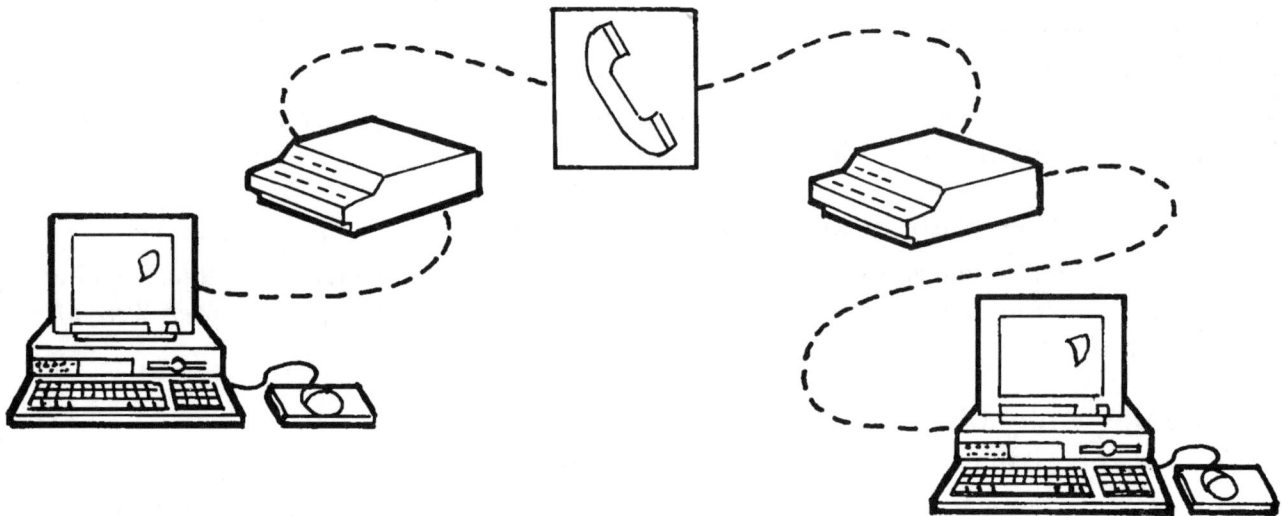

Storyboard Planning Sheet

Title Card

Button/Links: _____

Notes (Text/Sounds/Animations):
_____
_____

Table of Contents Card

Button/Links: _____

Notes (Text/Sounds/Animations):
_____
_____

Card 1

Button/Links: _____

Notes (Text/Sounds/Animations):
_____
_____

Card 2

Button/Links: _____

Notes (Text/Sounds/Animations):
_____
_____

Card 3

Button/Links: _____

Notes (Text/Sounds/Animations):
_____
_____

Card 4

Button/Links: _____

Notes (Text/Sounds/Animations):
_____
_____

Resources and Bibliography

Software

ClarisWorks 4.0. Claris Corporation, 1995.

Creative Writer. Microsoft Corporation, 1994.

HyperStudio. Roger Wagner Publishing, Inc., 1996.

Interactive Nova: Animal Pathfinders. Scholastic Software, 1991. (212) 505-3000.

The New Grolier Multimedia Encyclopedia: Release 6. Grolier, Inc., 1993.

Oregon Trail: Version 1.1. MECC, 1994. (612) 569-1500.

Point of View 2.0: An Overview of American History. *Point of View* is a trademark of Learningways, Inc. Available from Scholastic, Inc., 1993. (800) 541-5513.

Print Shop. Brøderbund Software, Inc., 1986.

SuperPrint. Scholastic, Inc., 1991.

Wagon Train 1848. MECC, 1997. (612) 569-1500.

WiggleWorks. Scholastic, Inc., 1994.

Writing Along the Oregon Trail. MECC, 1994. (612)569-1500.

Books

Blumberg, Rhoda. *The Great American Gold Rush*. Scholastic, Inc., 1989.

Moehle and Mitchell. *Westward Expansion*. Milliken Publishing Company.

Van Leeuwen, Jean. *Going West*. Dial Books for Young Readers, 1992.

The World Almanac for Kids: 1996. Funk & Wagnalls Corporation, 1995.

Online Services

America Online (800) 827-6364

CompuServ (800) 848-8990

Netscape (415) 254-1900

Prodigy (800) 776-3449 ext. 629

Net Search Providers

Excite, Yahoo, Infoseek, Lycos, Magellan